STICKER ADVENTURES

How to use this book

Read the captions, then find the sticker that best fits the space.
(Hint: check the sticker labels for clues!)

•

There are lots of fantastic extra stickers, too!

 Penguin Random House

Written by Julia March
Edited by Pamela Afram and Clare Millar
Designed by Radhika Banerjee, Karan Chaudhary, Elena Jarmoskaite,
and David McDonald
Cover designed by Mark Penfound

This edition published in 2018
First American Edition, 2015
First published in the United States by DK Publishing
345 Hudson Street, New York, New York 10014
DK, a Division of Penguin Random House LLC

001–310943–Oct/18

Page design copyright © 2018 Dorling Kindersley Limited.

LEGO, the LEGO logo, the Minifigure, and the Brick and Knob
configurations are trademarks and/or copyrights of the LEGO Group.
All rights reserved. ©2018 The LEGO Group.
Manufactured by Dorling Kindersley, 80 Strand, London,
WC2R 0RL under license from the LEGO Group.

Copyright © 2018 DC Comics.
All DC characters and elements © & ™ DC Comics.
(s18)

DORL41420

All rights reserved. Without limiting the rights under the copyright
reserved above, no part of this publication may be reproduced,
stored in or introduced into a retrieval system, or transmitted
in any form or by any means (electronic, mechanical, photocopying,
recording, or otherwise), without the prior written permission
of the copyright owner.

A catalog record for this book is available
from the Library of Congress.

ISBN: 978-1-4654-7656-2

Printed and bound in Heshan, China

www.LEGO.com
www.dccomics.com
www.dk.com

A WORLD OF IDEAS:
SEE ALL THERE IS TO KNOW

GOTHAM CITY

Gotham City is a dangerous place! Criminals, gangsters, and villains stalk its streets day and night. Batman has vowed to catch them all. He is determined to protect the good people who live in Gotham City.

BATMAN
Batman often fights crime after dark, and he usually wears black or very dark gray. No wonder people call him the Dark Knight!

ROBIN
Robin is Batman's faithful sidekick. The trusty teenager uses his martial arts skills to help Batman bring down villains.

WE NEED A HERO!

KEEPING WATCH
Batman and the Gotham City Police Department both work hard to rid the streets of crime.

BATGIRL

Batgirl is another crime fighter in Gotham City. Her costume hides her identity as Commissioner Gordon's daughter, Barbara.

COMMISSIONER GORDON

Meet Commissioner Gordon—chief of Gotham City Police Department. When he needs Batman's help, he beams the Bat-Signal into the sky.

NIGHTWING

Nightwing is an agile acrobat who sometimes helps Batman fight crime in Gotham City. His gauntlets conceal many weapons.

BATARANGS

Batman throws Batarangs at his enemies to stop them in their tracks! His fellow heroes carry similar weapons, too.

BATMOBILE

The Batmobile whizzes to the scene of a crime. The bat-symbol on the cockpit lets everyone know whose car it is!

BAT-SYMBOL

The bat-symbol is a yellow circle or oval containing the shape of a bat. If you see it, you will know that Batman is around.

FORCES OF EVIL

It is a tough job fighting crime in Gotham City. Around every corner is a villain desperate to defeat Batman. His enemies each have their own evil scheme planned out. The Dark Knight will need to outwit them all!

SCARECROW
Scarecrow may be smiling but he is far from friendly. He knows everyone's greatest fears and uses a special gas to scare his enemies.

MAN-BAT
Man-Bat uses a special serum to transform into a terrifying winged creature. He can navigate his way even in total darkness.

POISON IVY
Look out for Poison Ivy's dangerous vines! This leafy lady can control the minds of her enemies, and torment them with toxins.

BANE
Bane is extremely strong, and smart too. This tough enemy is highly trained in martial arts. He always wears a scary mask.

THE JOKER
This cunning villain is always grinning, but Batman does not find the Joker's evil plans funny. Crime is no joke!

©LEGO 2018

THE RIDDLER

The Riddler looks colorful in his green and purple suit. He loves confusing his victims with dastardly puzzles. Can Batman solve them?

©LEGO 2018

MR. FREEZE

This chilling scientist must wear a special suit or he will lose his cool! The suit also gives him super-strength and icy abilities.

©LEGO 2018

THE PENGUIN

The Penguin is very short but he wears a tall top hat. This dapper criminal loves birds and concocting evil schemes.

©LEGO 2018

RIDDLE ME THIS...

LET THE GOOD TIMES ROLL!

VILLAINOUS DUO

Oh no! When Batman's enemies team up, it means double trouble!

5

BATMAN VS BANE

Villains do not come any tougher than Bane. This muscle-bound martial artist was raised in prison. He spent his time strengthening his body and mind. Now he is free, he has set himself one challenge—to defeat Batman.

GORDON IN PERIL

Commissioner Gordon is in peril. Bane wants to capture him so Batman will come to his rescue. Then Bane can attack Batman!

BURLY BANE

Bane is very strong. He is even a bit stronger than Batman himself. He is also really smart, and can speak at least eight languages.

THE TUMBLER

Bane drives a fast, rugged vehicle called the Tumbler. He stole it from Batman and had it painted with his own designs.

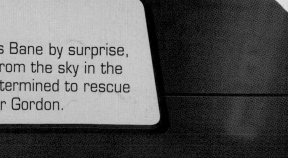

THE BAT

Batman takes Bane by surprise, swooping in from the sky in the Bat. He is determined to rescue Commissioner Gordon.

ROAD BARRIERS
There are barriers in the road, but Bane is not worried. The Tumbler is strong enough to bust through them without even slowing down.

©LEGO 2018

MISSILES
The Bat and the Tumbler are both equipped with missiles. The blue-tipped missiles go whistling through the air as Batman and Bane fire at each other.

RESCUE ROPE
When Batman gets close to Commissioner Gordon, he lowers the Bat's rescue rope. Gordon grabs it and Batman winches him up.

I WILL BEAT YOU, BATMAN!

ON BOARD
Made it! Commissioner Gordon is safe in his seat behind Batman in the Bat's cockpit. They fly away, leaving angry Bane behind.

TRY AGAIN, BANE
Bane has been beaten this time, but he is already hatching another plan to catch Batman.

FIGHTING CRIME

A walk through Gotham City can be a scary experience. Criminals are everywhere! Getaway cars speed around street corners and the sound of evil laughter fills the air. Luckily, Batman is around to stop them.

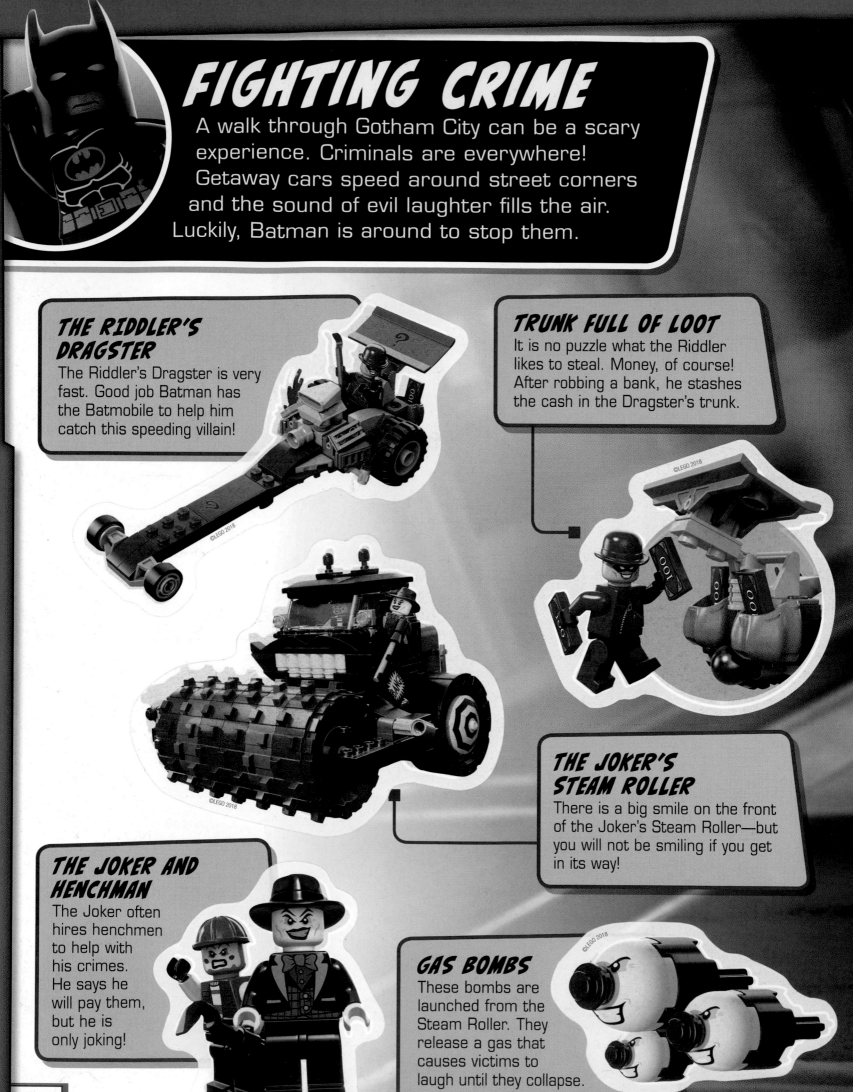

THE RIDDLER'S DRAGSTER

The Riddler's Dragster is very fast. Good job Batman has the Batmobile to help him catch this speeding villain!

TRUNK FULL OF LOOT

It is no puzzle what the Riddler likes to steal. Money, of course! After robbing a bank, he stashes the cash in the Dragster's trunk.

THE JOKER'S STEAM ROLLER

There is a big smile on the front of the Joker's Steam Roller—but you will not be smiling if you get in its way!

THE JOKER AND HENCHMAN

The Joker often hires henchmen to help with his crimes. He says he will pay them, but he is only joking!

GAS BOMBS

These bombs are launched from the Steam Roller. They release a gas that causes victims to laugh until they collapse.

EYES IN THE SKY
If the Dark Knight spots an ally in trouble, he winches them to safety in the Batcopter.

USE THE EXTRA STICKERS TO CREATE YOUR OWN SCENE HERE

WAR IN SMALLVILLE

Superman's home town of Smallville is being invaded by General Zod and his Kryptonian army! Their Black Zero Dropship casts a sinister shadow as it hovers over the city. Can Superman defeat these evil aliens?

MAN OF STEEL

Superman has happy memories of growing up in Smallville. He refuses to let the Kryptonians take over his home town!

LOIS LANE

Daily Planet journalist Lois Lane has escaped from General Zod once before. She doesn't want him to capture her again.

GENERAL ZOD

The power-hungry general wears a black and silver Kryptonian suit—and an evil scowl! His emblem is printed on his chest.

LETHAL COMBINATION

Faora and Tor-An are General Zod's two most trusted soldiers. Zod has ordered the pair to capture the Man of Steel.

©LEGO 2018

COLONEL HARDY

Colonel Nathan Hardy of the US Air Force arrives in his offroader. This brave soldier joins forces with Superman to fight the Kryptonians.

BLACK ZERO DROPSHIP

The Black Zero Dropship is ready for battle. It has dual shooters, a hidden weapon rack, and a rotating cannon underneath.

ESCAPE POD

Lois looks scared as her escape pod hurtles from the Black Zero Dropship. She is expecting a very bumpy landing!

SMALLVILLE IS MINE!

POWER CRAZY

General Zod wants power! He tried to take over Krypton and now he is trying to conquer the Earth.

KRYPTONIAN ARMOR

Earth's atmosphere could badly weaken General Zod. Protective armor and a helmet help him to retain his strength.

THE JUSTICE LEAGUE

When Super Heroes team up, it is enough to make any villain—human or alien—think twice. The Justice League is one of the world's most famous Super Hero teams—and with members like these, no wonder!

SUPERMAN

Superman was a founding member of the Justice League. He uses his powers of flight and super-strength to protect the innocent.

THE DARK KNIGHT

Batman is based in Gotham City but he will travel to join his Justice League teammates whenever they need him.

SEE YOU IN A FLASH!

ALWAYS ON TIME

When danger threatens, The Flash always arrives at a dash!

©LEGO 2018

©LEGO 2018

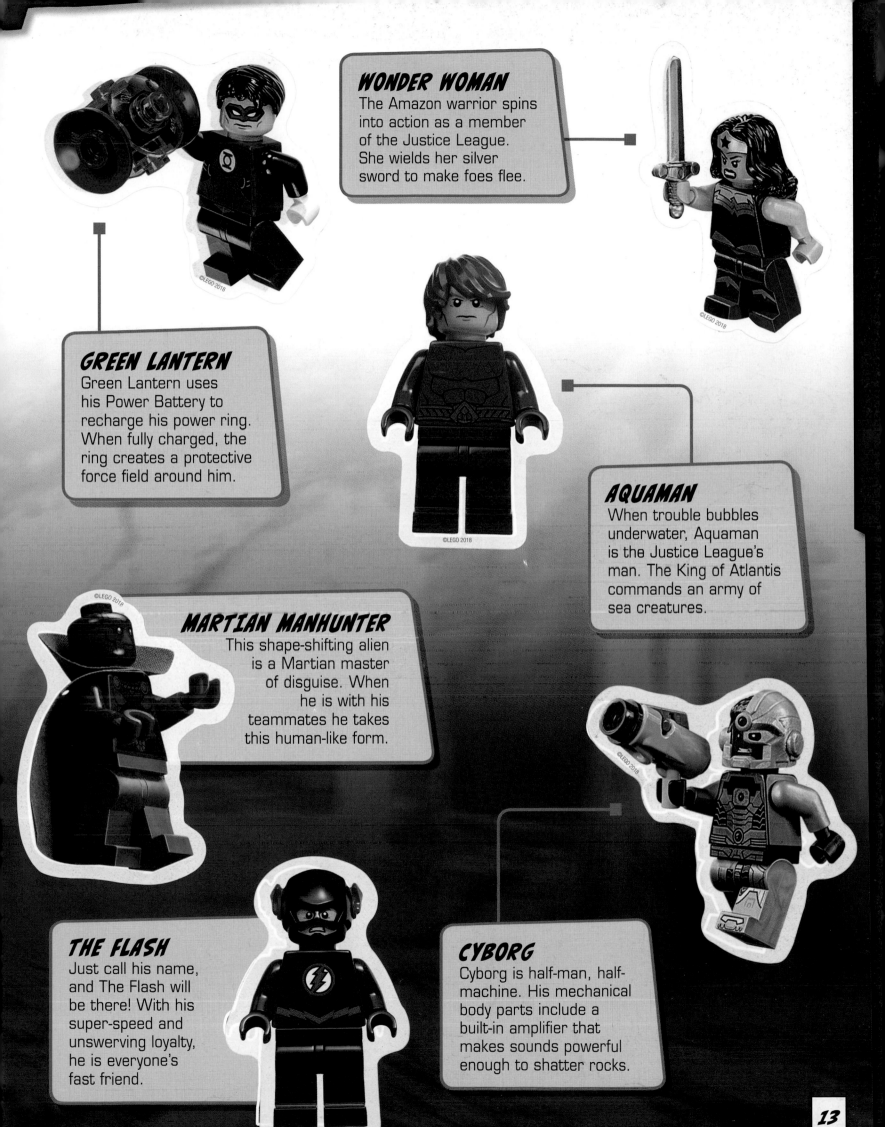

WONDER WOMAN

The Amazon warrior spins into action as a member of the Justice League. She wields her silver sword to make foes flee.

GREEN LANTERN

Green Lantern uses his Power Battery to recharge his power ring. When fully charged, the ring creates a protective force field around him.

AQUAMAN

When trouble bubbles underwater, Aquaman is the Justice League's man. The King of Atlantis commands an army of sea creatures.

MARTIAN MANHUNTER

This shape-shifting alien is a Martian master of disguise. When he is with his teammates he takes this human-like form.

THE FLASH

Just call his name, and The Flash will be there! With his super-speed and unswerving loyalty, he is everyone's fast friend.

CYBORG

Cyborg is half-man, half-machine. His mechanical body parts include a built-in amplifier that makes sounds powerful enough to shatter rocks.

13

ENEMIES OF JUSTICE

A host of horrible villains have taken on the Justice League. They all want to bring down this famous Super Hero team. But somehow the Justice League always come out on top. After all, they do have justice on their side.

I WILL DESTROY!

CAPTAIN COLD
When this cold commander aims his gun at the Justice League and yells "Freeze!" he really does want them to freeze.

GIANT THREAT
Darkseid can alter his size in an instant to tower over his enemies. Heads up, Justice League!

DARKSEID

Some of Darkseid's main foes are in the Justice League: Superman, Batman, and Wonder Woman. He would love to destroy all three.

GORILLA GRODD

Super-strong and super-smart, Gorilla Grodd is super bad-tempered too. The Justice League often have to rescue victims from his clutches.

BLACK MANTA

Black Manta wears a huge protective helmet. When the Justice League get too close he fires energy blasts at them from its eye sockets.

BRAINIAC

Brainiac is an alien android and an enemy of Superman. He is able to create multiple versions of himself.

SINESTRO

This sinister alien was once a Green Lantern, but he went bad and was sent into exile. He really hates the new Green Lantern.

CAPTAIN COLD'S GUN

A blast from Captain Cold's gun can cover the ground in ice. It is so slippery, even The Flash could lose his footing!

SINESTRO'S STAFF

Sinestro can create weapons like this staff just by using his thoughts. The powerful weapons he creates all glow a sickly yellow color.

DARING ESCAPE

Arkham Asylum is a dark and gloomy prison. The craziest, most dangerous criminals are locked up here to stop them from committing crimes. But some of them have escaped— and they are heading for Gotham City!

ARKHAM ASYLUM

Nobody likes visiting Arkham Asylum. The scary building has gargoyles and a spooky tower with a round red window.

©LEGO 2018

TRAPPED

While in this special cell, Poison Ivy can't use her toxins on guards, visitors, or other prisoners.

SECURITY VAN

The prisoners have hijacked this security vehicle and used it to escape from Arkham Asylum. Gotham City is about to receive some unwelcome guests!

HOLDING CELL

Scarecrow's name is printed on this cell. But he's nowhere to be found. He escaped in the security van!

©LEGO 2018

ARKHAM ASYLUM
GOTHAM CITY

28MB89

SCARECROW

©LEGO 2018

BRAVE BATMAN
Batman will capture escaped prisoners and will bring them back to Arkham Asylum. Gotham City will be safe again!

MEDICAL ROOM
Dr. Harleen Quinzel treats prisoners in the medical room. She has spent many hours here trying to cure the Joker of his insanity.

SECRET IDENTITY
Dr. Quinzel has gone a little crazy. She is now the Joker's girlfriend, Harley Quinn! She keeps her costume well hidden.

PRISON GUARD
This prison guard is ready to handcuff the prisoners. Some of them are back in their cells already. Phew!

AMAZING ALLIES

Sometimes even Super Heroes need someone to come to their rescue! Luckily, there is a whole host of champions who would risk their own lives to help out a friend in a fix.

SHARP SHOT

Green Arrow's allies are always happy when he appears at their side in a battle. They know this sharp shot never misses his target!

ALIEN ALLY

Martian Manhunter protects his friends by using telekinesis to push away any missiles fired at them.

WINGED WARRIOR

When Hawkman spots an ally in a trap, he swoops in from above wielding his mighty mace and comes to their rescue!

SUPERGIRL

Supergirl is from Krypton, and has powers similar to Superman's. She is loyal to her allies too, just like Superman.

ARKHAM GUARD

He may not have superpowers, but this prison guard is a true hero. He keeps dangerous felons away from the public.

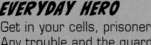

EVERYDAY HERO

Get in your cells, prisoners! Any trouble and the guard will call Batman!

USE THE EXTRA STICKERS TO CREATE YOUR OWN SCENE HERE

TIME FOR ACTION

Super Heroes are not all the same. Each has a unique ability they can call on to challenge their foes. Whatever the crisis, there is always a Super Hero with the perfect skills to win the battle.

BATARANG GIRL

Batgirl is an expert in throwing Batarangs. These shuriken-like weapons return to her after hitting their target.

HIGH-FLYING HERO

Hawkman's wings are made from mysterious Nth Metal. They enable him to swoop in on enemies from the skies.

POWERFUL PRINCESS

Wonder Woman is a warrior princess of the Amazons. She wears a tiara that can also be used as a weapon against her enemies.

ACE ARCHER

Green Arrow is the most accurate archer in the world. He has created a range of trick arrows each designed to combat a different foe.

EMERALD WARRIOR

Green Lantern has the power to create any object he can imagine. The objects are made out of green light.

STRENGTH OF WILL

Green Lantern can create any weapon just by willing it into existence. But if his willpower wavers it will disappear!

NO EVIL SHALL ESCAPE MY SIGHT!

QUICK TO ACT

The Flash can run at the speed of light, but that is not all! He can think, react, read, and even speak at light speed!

KING OF THE WAVES

Aquaman wields the Trident of Neptune. With it he can whip up tidal waves, whirlpools, and sea storms to make his foes flounder.

UP, UP, AND AWAY

Flying is easy for Superman because Earth's gravity is too weak to pull him down. He also gets his power from the sun!

©LEGO 2018

21

POWER SUITS

Batman is most often seen in his classic Batsuit, but it is not his only costume. In fact, the Dark Knight has a number of Batsuits in his closet. Each of them is perfectly suited for a different situation.

WINGED SAVIOR
This rare version of the Batsuit does not have a cape. Instead, it has stiff wings that enable Batman to glide short distances.

I'M READY TO SAVE THE WORLD!

ARCTIC BATMAN
When fighting Mr. Freeze in the Arctic, Batman wears this white Batsuit. It helps to camouflage him against the snow.

COWLED CRUSADER
All Batman's suits have a bat-eared cowl. It helps to hide his identity as Bruce Wayne.

22

GRAY SUIT

Batman wore this dark gray Batsuit when he fought Bane in Gotham City. He kept his usual black cowl, though.

©LEGO 2018

©LEGO 2018

©LEGO 2018

CLASSIC BATSUIT

Batman puts on his classic suit for everyday crime fighting. It is black with a yellow bat-symbol and Utility Belt.

WATERWEAR

Underwater battles are no problem for Batman in this sleek blue scuba suit with an air tank. The Dark Knight is a sure shot with that harpoon!

©LEGO 2018

DIVING GEAR

Robin is never out of his depth in this deep sea dive suit. It has an unlimited supply of air.

©LEGO 2018

READY FOR SPACE

Batman went into space to fight evil genius Brainiac wearing this silver space suit. It has an air tank and jointed metal wings.

CLOAKED ROBIN

When going undercover, Robin pulls on a hooded cloak. It keeps his face in shadow and partly hides his red tunic.

©LEGO 2018

THE POWER OF EVIL

Villains will try anything to destroy the Super Heroes who try to put an end to their evil plans. Whether it's an ice-cold blast or a toxic draft, sometimes they can come dangerously close to success.

COLD ENEMY

Mr. Freeze's gun fires an icy stream that immobilizes his enemies. He hopes his victims will have an ice day!

IT'S TIME TO COOL YOU DOWN!

COLD HEARTED

Only one thing might warm Mr. Freeze's heart: seeing Batman in a bat-shaped block of ice.

©LEGO 2018

ROBOT PENGUINS

The Penguin plans to send this remote-controlled robotic penguin with his stick of dynamite to sneak up on Batman!

©LEGO 2018

TRICK UMBRELLA

The Penguin always carries an umbrella, but he doesn't mind the rain. The umbrella actually hides a variety of weapons, like this powerful gun.

TOXIC TOUCH

Poison Ivy usually subdues foes with her plant-based toxins. But sometimes she ties them up with a piece of stringy weed instead!

RIDDLE ME THIS

There is one puzzle even the Riddler can't solve. How does Batman keep escaping from his wily traps?

EVIL TYRANT

Even Super Heroes avoid looking Darkseid in the face. The Omega Beam he fires from his eyes might blow them to bits.

BOMBS AWAY!

Man-Bat is having a blast throwing his packs of powerful dynamite at his rivals. Watch out!

TELEPATHIC APE

Gorilla Grodd keeps trying to take over The Flash's mind, but The Flash thinks so fast that Grodd can't keep up!

ENEMY VEHICLES

Villains are always inventing special vehicles to help them when they need to escape. They think they are in the driving seat, but Batman, Superman, and their allies always find a way to put the brakes on their evil plans.

ROBOSHARK

Black Manta's Roboshark is highly dangerous. It can't bite anything, but it has lethal lasers on either side of its fin.

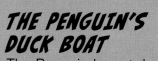

SEA SAUCER

Black Manta waits on the seabed in his red Sea Saucer ready to attack Batman with the vehicle's deadly shooters!

THE PENGUIN'S DUCK BOAT

The Penguin has stolen a valuable diamond. He is making a quack getaway in this duck-shaped boat!

HOVER DESTROYER

Heroes beware! Darkseid's Hover Destroyer is fitted with a swiveling cannon. It blasts out cannonballs with terrific power.

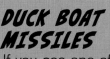

DUCK BOAT MISSILES

If you see one of these orange-tipped missiles heading toward you, there is only one thing to do—duck!

USE THE EXTRA
STICKERS TO
CREATE YOUR OWN
SCENE HERE

GORILLA ATTACK

Gorilla Grodd is attacking Gotham City! He wants to get his hands on every banana in town. To make matters worse, Captain Cold has joined in, causing mayhem. It's enough to drive a Super Hero bananas!

BANANA TRUCK
Gorilla Grodd has stopped a banana truck. Fruit stores all over Gotham City will not get their deliveries. Can the Super Heroes help?

FAST RESPONSE
The ape's old enemy The Flash is first on the scene as usual, but he needs back-up. Don't worry— Batman is on his way.

GORILLA GRAB!
Grodd is grabbing the bananas, and if anyone gets in his way he is grabbing them, too! The banana truck driver is his first victim.

BANANA TRUCK DRIVER
This banana truck driver didn't expect this when he loaded up his truck this morning. He is glad to see Batman!

28

IT'S CAPE VERSUS APE!

©LEGO 2018

BANANAS OR BUST!
Batman takes every mission seriously, even if it is just bananas at risk.

FROSTY FOE
Captain Cold doesn't care about bananas. He has come to town for a chance to defeat his arch- enemy, The Flash.

BAT·MECH
Batman is in his awesome Bat-Mech. He can fire its net to trap Grodd, then use its Super Jumper to launch himself at the ape.

CRATE CRUSADER
Grodd has been caught and the bananas are back in their crates. Time for the Dark Knight to slip back to the Batcave!

29

AIR STRIKE

Some villains aim high. They use flying machines to commit crimes or to attack their enemies from the skies. But the Super Heroes have their own incredible vehicles. Some don't even need machines to fly!

SUPER FLYER

Superman soars through the skies faster than a speeding bullet. He will put a stop to the villains' airborne antics.

BATCOPTER

Batman chases wrongdoers through the skies in his Batcopter. It has a grapple hook for snatching up the villains below it.

FAST FLYER

Hawkman flaps his wings or uses them to glide through the sky. He controls his wings using just the power of his mind.

GREEN LANTERN SPACESHIP

Green Lantern speeds into battle in his sleek green spaceship. It has a Green Lantern symbol on the nose.

©LEGO 2018

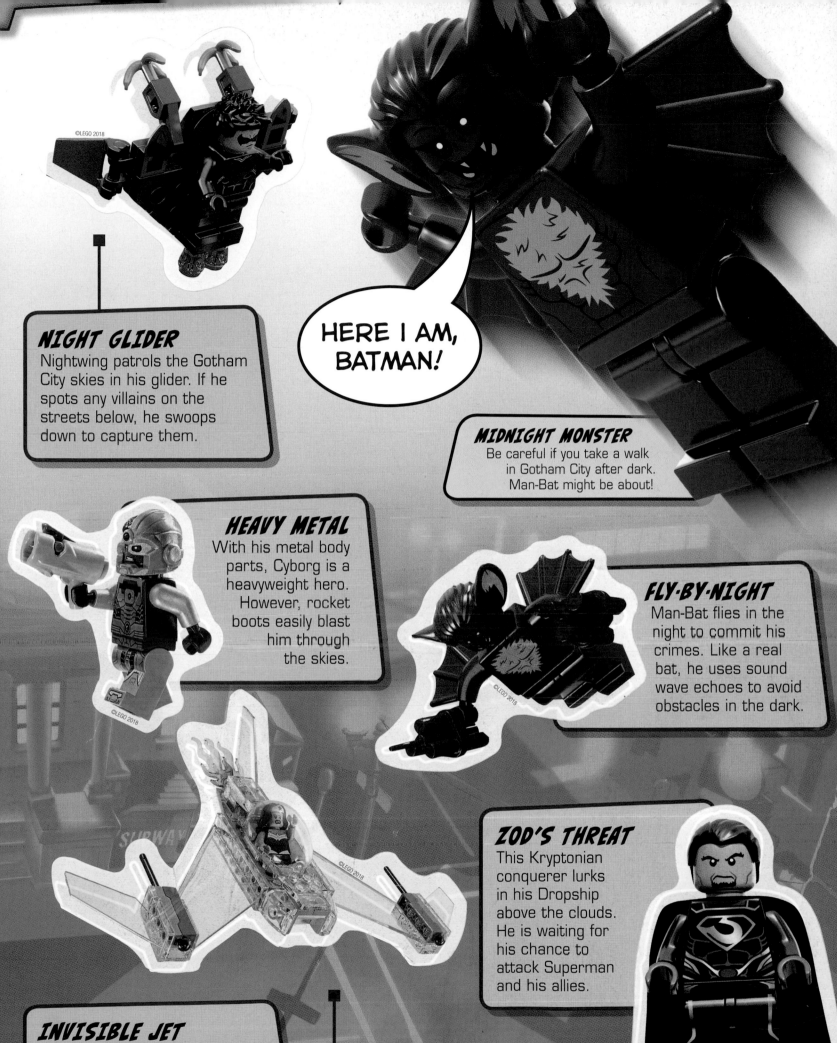

NIGHT GLIDER
Nightwing patrols the Gotham City skies in his glider. If he spots any villains on the streets below, he swoops down to capture them.

HERE I AM, BATMAN!

MIDNIGHT MONSTER
Be careful if you take a walk in Gotham City after dark. Man-Bat might be about!

HEAVY METAL
With his metal body parts, Cyborg is a heavyweight hero. However, rocket boots easily blast him through the skies.

FLY-BY-NIGHT
Man-Bat flies in the night to commit his crimes. Like a real bat, he uses sound wave echoes to avoid obstacles in the dark.

ZOD'S THREAT
This Kryptonian conquerer lurks in his Dropship above the clouds. He is waiting for his chance to attack Superman and his allies.

INVISIBLE JET
Wonder Woman flies an Invisible Jet. Foes won't see her coming until she jumps out and surprises them!

31

UNDERWATER KING

Aquaman rules the undersea city of Atlantis. All sea creatures obey his commands. When danger threatens his city, Aquaman wields his golden trident to whisk up whirlpools, tidal waves, and bursts of crackling lightning!

FROZEN IN ICE
Mr. Freeze has frozen Aquaman in a block of ice. The King of Atlantis can't even wield his trident!

©LEGO 2018

ICE BREAKER
Batman fires bombs at the ice block prison. When they explode, the ice block splits in two. Aquaman is free!

©LEGO 2018

MANTA MENACE
Black Manta thinks he should rule the seas instead of Aquaman. He carries a gleaming silver spear.

©LEGO 2018

I CONTROL THE SEVEN SEAS!

SCUBA BATMAN
Aquaman's ally, Batman, can't breathe under water. He has to wear a special Batsuit that is fitted with an air tank.

GOLDEN HERO
Aquaman is one of only a few Atlanteans who were born with golden hair.

©LEGO 2018

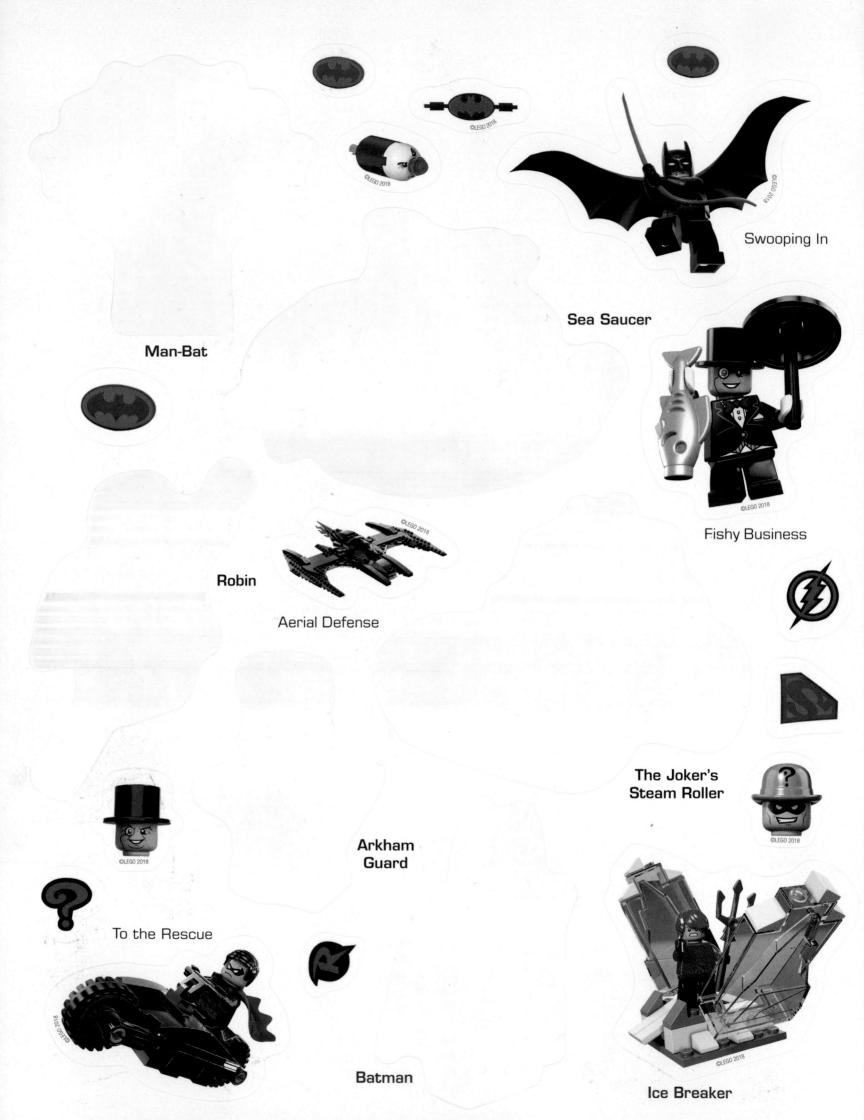

Swooping In

Sea Saucer

Man-Bat

Fishy Business

Robin

Aerial Defense

The Joker's
Steam Roller

Arkham
Guard

To the Rescue

Batman

Ice Breaker

TM & © DC Comics. (s18)

Patrolling the Skies

Winged Warrior

The Joker's Joke Gun

A Duck Boat Ride

Captain Cold's Gun

Sharp Shot

Fighting Crime

POW

Nightwing

Taking Aim

The Riddler

Green Lantern

Henchman

Batmobile

Scary Scarecrow

TM & © DC Comics. (s18)

Winged Savior

Batcave

Batarangs

Supergirl

The Penguin

King of the
Seven Seas

Strong
Superman

Escaping Zod

The Joker

Hardy the Hero

Caped Crusader

Batman Flying to
the Rescue

Cyborg

TM & © DC Comics. (s18)

Diving Gear

Batgirl

Scarecrow

Frozen in Ice

Go
Figure!

Gray Suit

Robin Fighting

Speedy
Vehicle

Flying Kick

Defying Gravity

Hover
Destroyer

Gorilla Grodd

TM & © DC Comics. (s18)

Penguin Bomb

Ready for Space

POW

Bat-symbol

Fast Response

Holding Cell

Crate Crusader

R

Up, Up, And Away

The Batboat

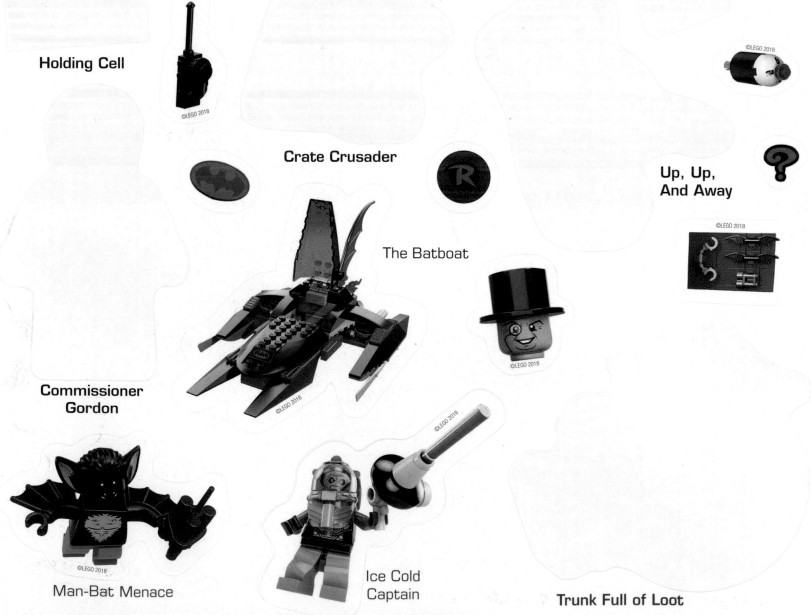

Commissioner Gordon

Man-Bat Menace

Ice Cold Captain

Trunk Full of Loot

TM & © DC Comics. (s18)

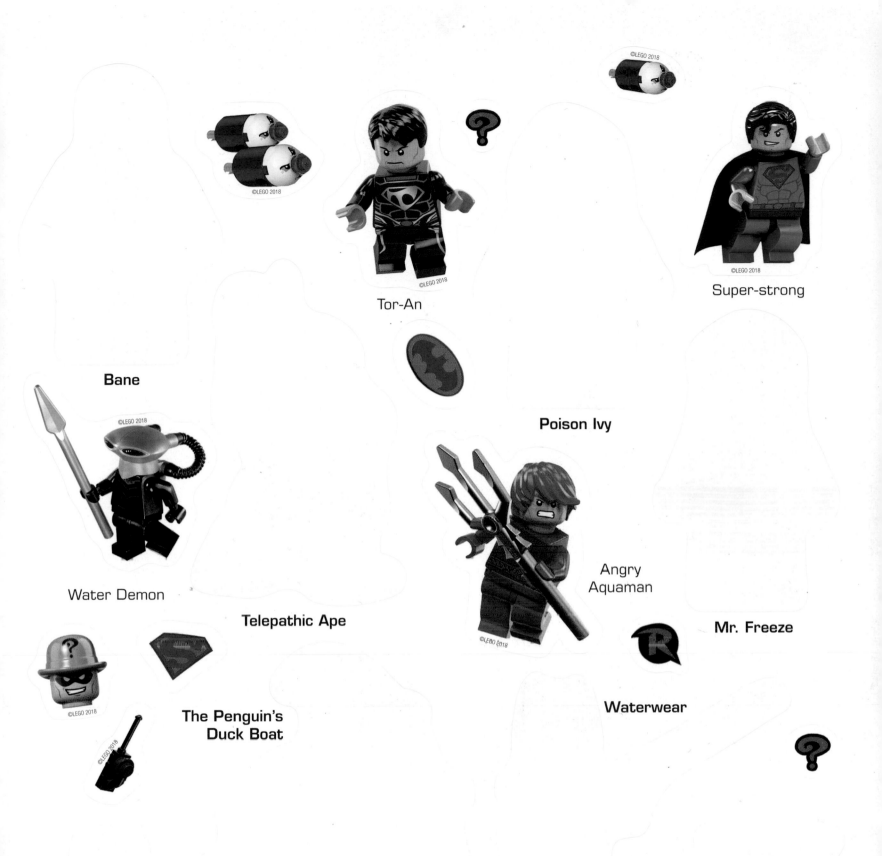

Tor-An

Super-strong

Bane

Poison Ivy

Water Demon

Angry Aquaman

Telepathic Ape

Mr. Freeze

The Penguin's Duck Boat

Waterwear

Arctic Batman

Duck Boat Missiles

The Riddler's Dragster

TM & © DC Comics. (s18)

Swooping In

The Dapper Penguin

Wonder Woman

Ace Archer

Scuba Batman

Cloaked Robin

Alien Ally

Emerald Warrior

The Batwing Takes Flight

Brutal Bane

Roboshark

Bat-Mech

TM & © DC Comics. (s18)

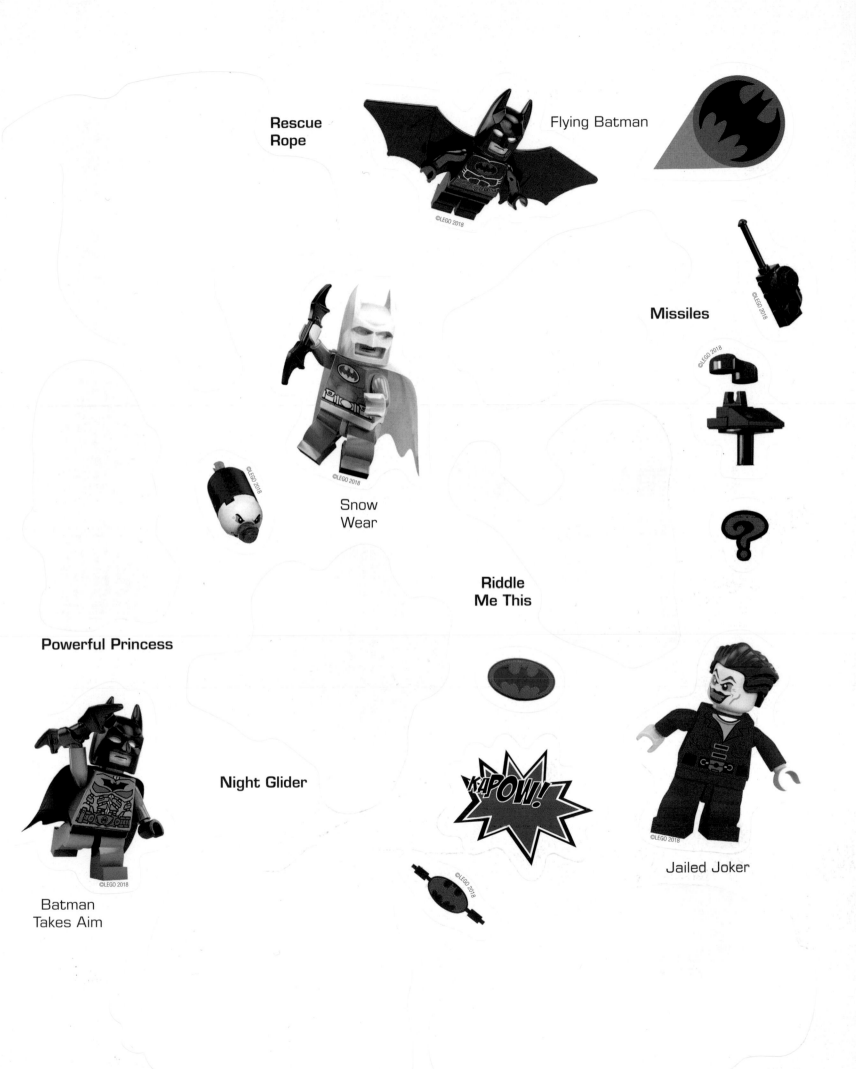

Rescue
Rope

Flying Batman

Missiles

Snow
Wear

Riddle
Me This

Powerful Princess

Night Glider

Jailed Joker

KAPOW!

Batman
Takes Aim

High-Flying
Hero

The Tumbler

TM & © DC Comics. (s18)

Darkseid

Road Barriers

Gordon in Peril

Trick Shot

Prison Guard

Fly-By-Night

Sinestro

Manta's
Spear

**Trick
Umbrella**

Frosty Foe

Burly Bane

Bat Vehicle

TM & © DC Comics. (s18)

Escape Pod

Man of Steel

Batcopter

Secret Identity

Evil Tyrant

Brainiac

Colonel Hardy

Angry Robin

Robot Penguins   **General Zod**   **Martian Manhunter**   **Trapped**

TM & © DC Comics. (s18)

Classic Batsuit

Plant Queen

Captain Cold

Black Manta

Kryptonian Armor

Glide Attack

Lethal Combination

Quick to Act

Medical Room

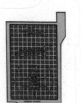

Superman

Moonlit Hero

TM & © DC Comics. (s18)

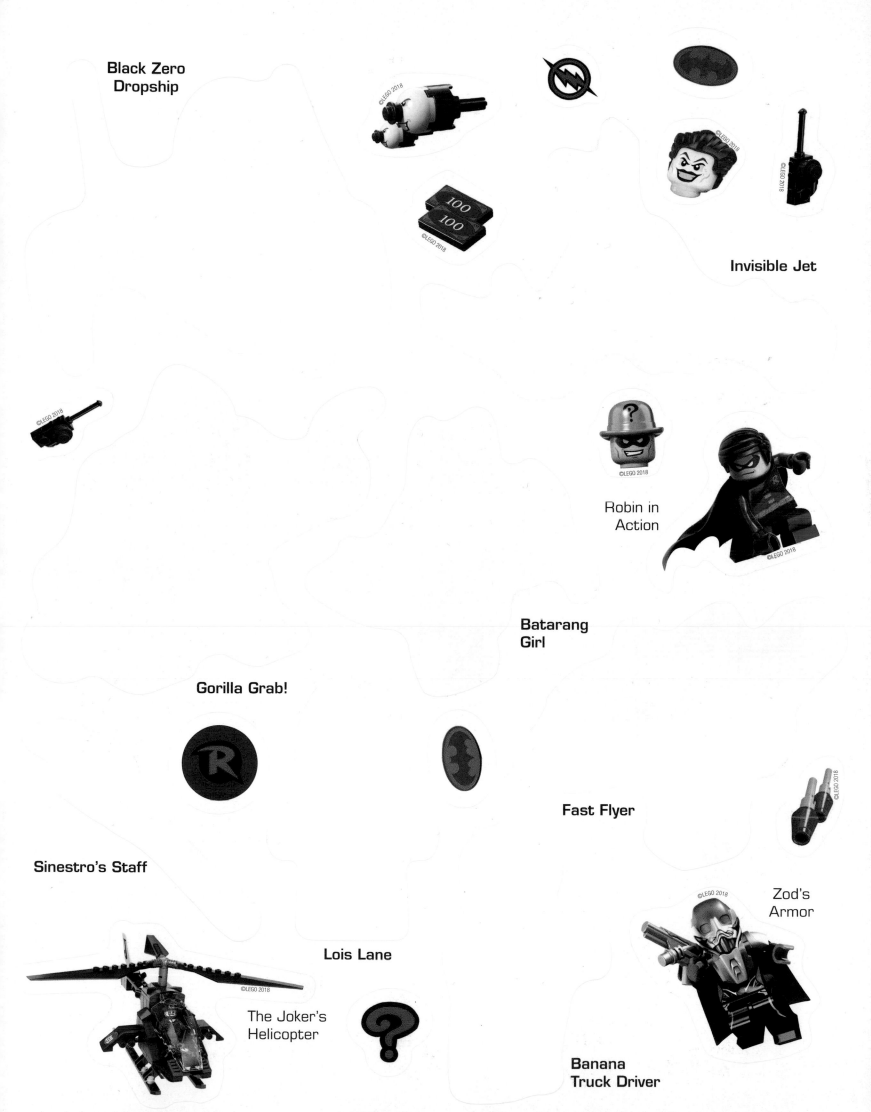

Black Zero
Dropship

Invisible Jet

Robin in
Action

Batarang
Girl

Gorilla Grab!

Fast Flyer

Sinestro's Staff

Zod's
Armor

Lois Lane

The Joker's
Helicopter

Banana
Truck Driver

TM & © DC Comics. (s18)

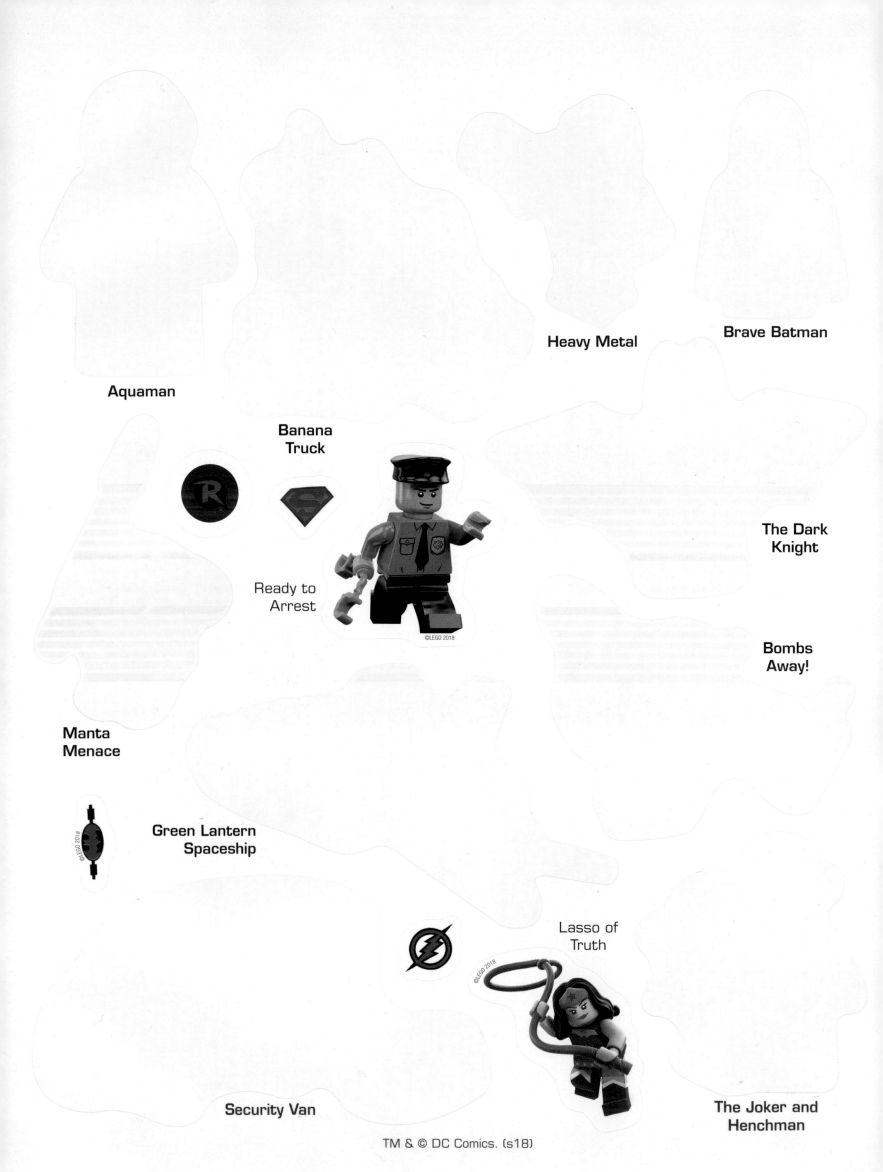

Heavy Metal

Brave Batman

Aquaman

Banana
Truck

The Dark
Knight

Ready to
Arrest

Bombs
Away!

Manta
Menace

Green Lantern
Spaceship

Lasso of
Truth

Security Van

The Joker and
Henchman

TM & © DC Comics. (s18)

King of
the Waves

On Board

Arkham Asylum

Gas Bombs

Cold Enemy

Earth's Protector

Zod's Threat

Super Flyer

The Bat

The Flash

Toxic
Touch

TM & © DC Comics. (s18)

Extra Stickers

TM & © DC Comics. (s18)

Extra Stickers

© 2018 LEGO   TM & © DC Comics. (s18)

© 2018 LEGO   TM & © DC Comics. (s18)

© 2018 LEGO TM & © DC Comics. (s18)

© 2018 LEGO   TM & © DC Comics. (s18)

© 2018 LEGO   TM & © DC Comics. (s18)

©2018 The LEGO Group
TM & © 2018 DC Comics. (s18)

©2018 The LEGO Group
TM & © 2018 DC Comics. (s18)